WISDOM WEAVERS

Explore the Ojibwe Language and the Meaning of Dream Catchers

James Vukelich Kaagegaabaw
Illustrated by Marcus Trujillo

becker&mayer! kids

THE HISTORY OF THE OJIBWE LANGUAGE

The history of the Ojibwe language goes back hundreds of years. Also called Anishinaabemowin, this language is spoken by the Ojibwe people, who are native to the area around the Great Lakes in North America.

The Ojibwe people have a strong tradition of sharing knowledge, customs, and stories through their language. When settlers came to North America, they tried to make Ojibwe people speak English and forget their traditions. But even during these hard times, the Ojibwe language and culture stayed alive in their communities.

THE DREAM CATCHER TRADITION

Dreams are very important spiritually and culturally to Ojibwe people throughout their lives. An *izhi'on*, or dream catcher, is made for an Ojibwe baby to protect them. The web in the dream catcher would let the good dreams pass through and capture the nightmares. The web can also show a baby (who is just starting to learn by watching) how they are connected to everything and everyone around them, with their relatives, and the world.

As the baby grows and becomes a child and then a teen, they may seek out a dream during what is called a Vision Quest. They may fast—stop eating and drinking—for a period of days in order to dream. They may receive a dream or vision that will help and guide them through life. As adults and elders, Ojibwe may dream as a way of learning about both the seen and the unseen worlds (the world we live in and the spirit world) and share that with the community.

And so, from birth through all periods of life, the idea of the dream holds a special place in Ojibwe tradition and culture.

HOW TO USE THIS BOOK

Follow Jack as he spends a day learning about his Ojibwe family and traditions. From morning to afternoon, through evening and night, Jack learns Ojibwe words for everyday things and the history behind the dream catcher.

See if you can find these words on every page in both the Ojibwe language and English, with guides on how to correctly say each word in Ojibwe.

Pay close attention and look for the special words and phrases next to the icon of the dream catcher.

Ojibwe spelling

QR Code

Mino-giizhigad
Mi-no gee-zhi-gud
It is a good day.

Ojibwe pronunciation

English meaning

Scan the QR code with your smartphone to hear how they sound! At the back of the book, find even more words in Ojibwe with codes to scan—hear how they sound and learn to say them.

"*Mino-giizhigad*. Good morning, Jack! Time to get ready for school!"

"Oh man," Jack yawned. "I was having THE BEST dream."

"*Howah!* Wow! That must be working," said Dad, looking at the dream catcher on the wall.

Giizis
gee-zis
Sun

Waasechigan
wah-say-chi-gun
Window

Mitig
mi-tig
Tree

Mino-giizhigad
Mi-no gee-zhi-gud
It is a good day.

Nibaagan
ni-bah-gun
Bed

Odaminwaagan
o-da-minwah-gun
Toy

"What do you mean?" asked Jack.

"An *izhi'on* lets the good dreams through and catches the bad ones. I made this for you before you were born, as many Ojibwe parents do for their children. It is tradition," Dad explained.

Jack looked closer at the dream catcher. "Cool! What's for breakfast?"

Waazakonenjigan
wah-zu-ko-nayn-ji-gun
Lamp

Apikweshimon
a-pi-kway-shi-mon
Pillow

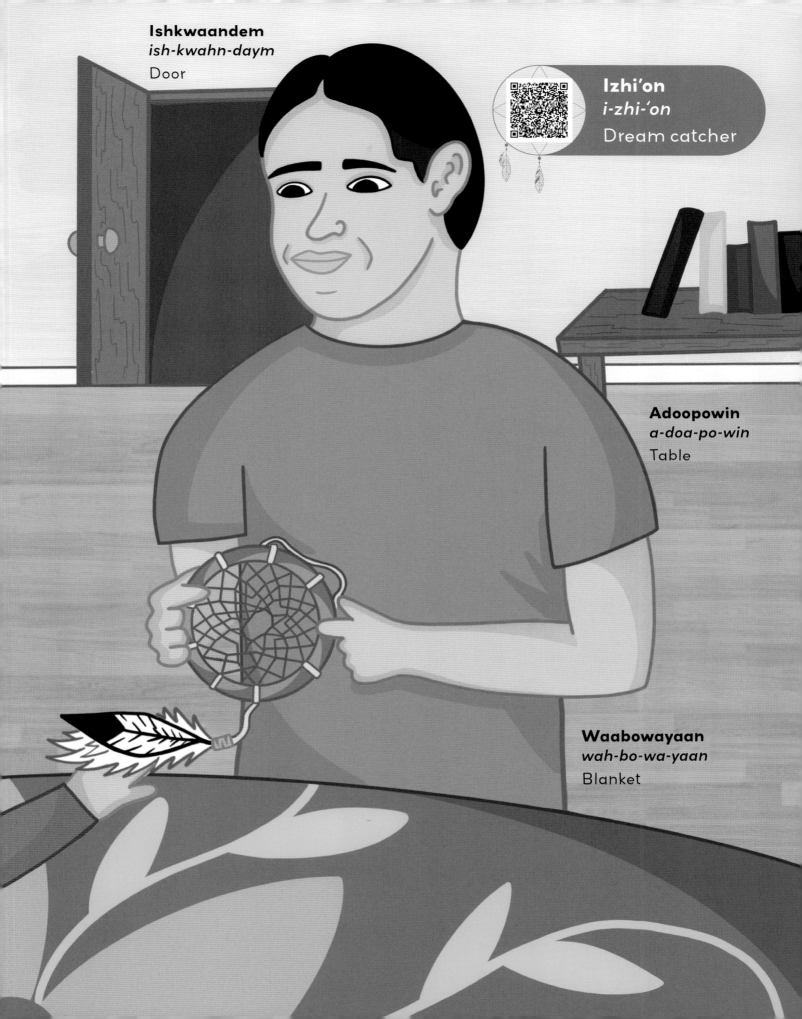

Ishkwaandem
ish-kwahn-daym
Door

Izhi'on
i-zhi-'on
Dream catcher

Adoopowin
a-doa-po-win
Table

Waabowayaan
wah-bo-wa-yaan
Blanket

As Jack got out of the car at school, Dad said the same thing he said every morning.

"*Giga-waabamin, gizhawenimin.*"

"*Giga-waabamin, gizhawenimin!*" Jack replied.

At school that day, Jack and the other *gikinoo'amaagan* learned about dream catchers.

"I know all about these!" beamed Jack. "I've had one since before I was born." He felt proud to share this news about his Ojibwe tradition with his class.

Apibii'igan
a-pi-bee-'-i-gun
Desk

Minikwaajigan
mi-ni-kwah-chi-gun
Mug

Gikinoo'amaagan
gih-kin-new-ah-mah-gun
Students

Mazina'igan
ma-zi-na-'-i-gun
Book

Gekinoo'amaaged
gay-kin-new-'a-mah-gayd
Teacher

Ozhibii'iganaak
o-zhi-bee-'-i-gun-ahk
Pencil

When Jack got home after school, Dad was waiting with a surprise.

"*Maajaadaa*," Dad said. "Come on, Jack. We're going on an adventure!"

They packed snacks and supplies and started out on their hike down to the lake.

Bimiwanaan
bi-mi-wu-nahn
Backpack

Miijim
me-jim
Food

Miikana
me-kuh-nuh
Trail

Maajaadaa
mah-jah-dah
Let's go!

Aanakwad
ah-nuh-kwud
Clouds

Zaaga'igan
zah-ga-'-i-gun
Lake

"We'll make a dream catcher, starting with red willow for the frame," Dad said.

"Before harvesting, we always speak to the plant and make an offering of tobacco, one of the four Sacred Plants, to say *miigwech* to nature for its gifts."

Giigoonh
gee-gohn
Fish

"It's important to make the hoop right after the *miskwaabiimizh* is harvested, while it's flexible so it doesn't break," Dad said as he carefully shaped the red willow branch.

"The round shape represents the circle of life."

Ingozis
in-go-zihs
Son

Moozhwaagan
moozsh-wah-gun
Scissors

Asabaab
uh-sub-ahb
String

Miskwaabiimizh
mih-skwah-bee-mizh
Red willow

Indede
in-day-day
Father

Waawiyeyaa
wah-we-yay-yah
It is a circle.

"Let's lace this up! We'll add seven loops, which represent the Seven Grandfather Teachings: Truth, Honesty, Humility, Respect, Courage, Wisdom, and most importantly, *Zaagi'idiwin.*"

Zaagi'idiwin
zah-gih-'-ih-dih-win
Love

Nibwaakaawin
nih-bwah-kah-win
Wisdom

Debwewin
day-bway-win
Truth

Zoongide'ewin
zoon-gih-day-ay-win
Bravery

Gwayakwaadiziwin
gwhy-ahk-wah-dih-zih-win
Honesty

Manaaji'idiwin
muh-nah-ji-dih-win
Respect

Dabasendizowin
duh-buh-sayn-dih-zoh-win
Humility

"Now we will tie a *miigwan* in the center," Dad said. "It symbolizes our spiritual connection with the Ojibwe people and all of our relatives, from now and in the past."

Jack helped by picking out a few *manidoominens* in his favorite colors to add for decoration.

Onaagoshin
oh-NAH-go-shin
It is evening.

Manidoo
ma-nih-doo
Spirit

Jack looked up and noticed something shining in the sky.

"Dad, it's the Big Dipper! Look, it's leading the way to that one really bright *anang*."

"Yes, just like the Seven Grandfather Teachings, seven stars make up the Great Fisher," said Dad. "And it always points to the North Star."

Dibiki-giizis
dih-bih-kih gee-zis
Moon

Dibikad
dih-bih-kud
It is night.

Anang
a-nung
Star

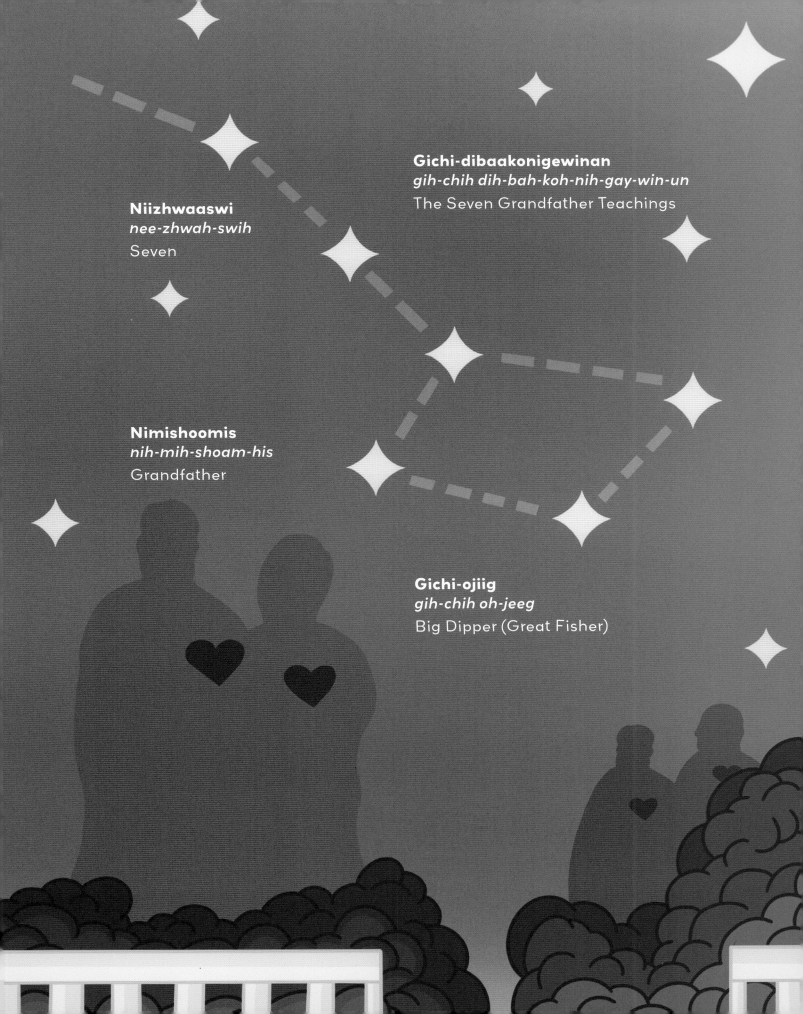

Niizhwaaswi
nee-zhwah-swih
Seven

Gichi-dibaakonigewinan
gih-chih dih-bah-koh-nih-gay-win-un
The Seven Grandfather Teachings

Nimishoomis
nih-mih-shoam-his
Grandfather

Gichi-ojiig
gih-chih oh-jeeg
Big Dipper (Great Fisher)

"Let's hang this dream catcher in Grandma's room as a *miigiwewin*," Dad said. "It can catch all of the good dreams for her when she spends the night with us."

Nookomis
no-koh-mihs
Grandmother

Apabiwin
a-pa-bi-win
Chair

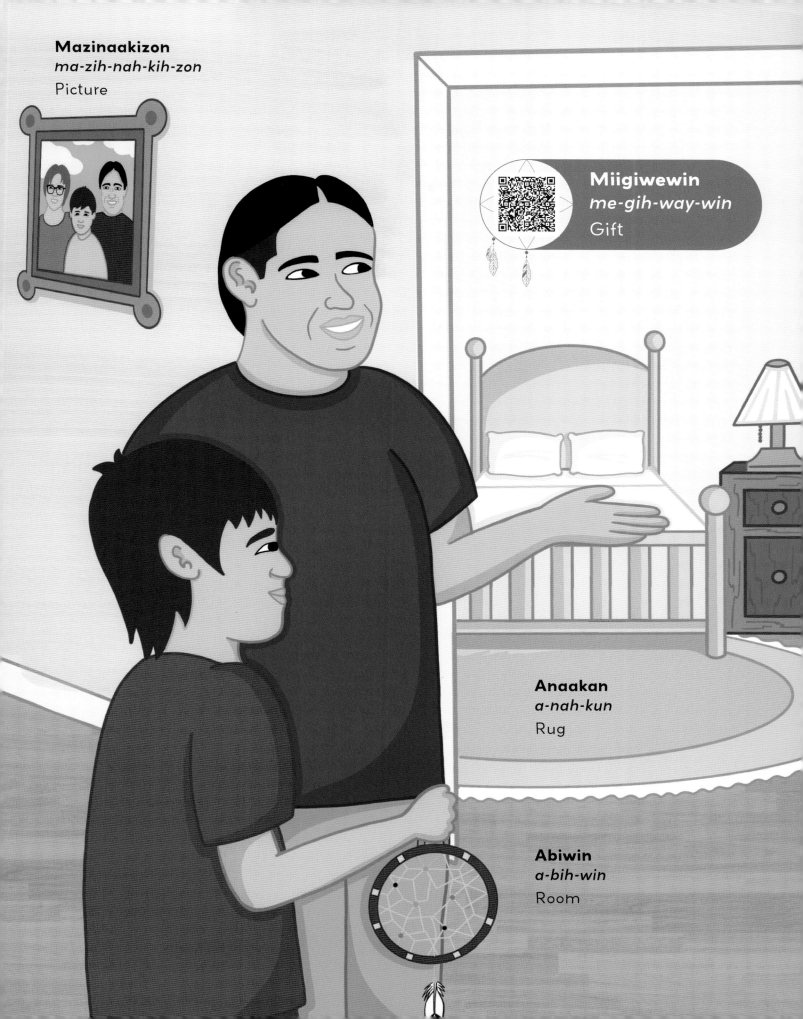

Mazinaakizon
ma-zih-nah-kih-zon
Picture

Miigiwewin
me-gih-way-win
Gift

Anaakan
a-nah-kun
Rug

Abiwin
a-bih-win
Room

After a long day of learning so many amazing things, Jack sleepily climbed into bed.

"Good night, Jack!" Dad said. "I love you, sleep well."

"Good night, Dad," Jack replied as he drifted off to sleep.

And that night, snuggled safely under his dream catcher, Jack *bawaajige* about each *indaanikoobijigan* and all of his family.

Bawaajige
ba-wah-jih-gay
S/he dreams.

Indaanikoobijigan
in-dah-nih-koh-bih-jih-gun

Ancestor

LEARN MORE WORDS IN OJIBWE TO USE THROUGHOUT YOUR DAY!

Scan the codes to hear how to say the words correctly.

MORNING

 Nibaagan
Bed

 Apikweshimon
Pillow

 Gikinoo'amaadiiwigamig
School

 Odaminwaagan
Toy

 Adoopowin
Table

 Abinoojiinh
Child

 Waasechigan
Window

 Waabowayaan
Blanket

 Bineshiinh
Bird

 Mitig
Tree

 Waazakonenjigan
Lamp

 Odaabaan
Car

 Giizis
Sun

 Ishkwaandem
Door

 Animosh
Dog

AFTERNOON

 Apibii'igan
Desk

 Aanakwad
Clouds

 Biindaakoojige
Offering

 Mazina'igan
Book

 Bimiwanaan
Backpack

 Giigoonh
Fish

 Ozhibii'iganaak
Pencil

 Miijim
Food

 Waabooz
Rabbit

 Minikwaajigan
Mug

 Miikana
Trail

 Asemaa
Tobacco

 Gekinoo'amaaged
Teacher

 Zaaga'igan
Lake

Waawiyeyaa
It is a circle.

Debwewin
Truth

Manidoominens
Beads

Asabaab
String

Gwayakwaadiziwin
Honesty

Nimaamaa
Mother

Moozhwaagan
Scissors

Dabasendizowin
Humility

Apiitendaasozi
S/he is important.

Indede
Father

Manaaji'idiwin
Respect

Manidoo
Spirit

Ingozis
Son

Zoongide'ewin
Bravery

Onaagoshin
It is evening.

Dibikad
It is night.

Nibwaakaawin
Wisdom

Niizhwaaswi
Seven

Nookomis
Grandmother

Nibaa
S/he sleeps.

Nimishoomis
Grandfather

Abiwin
Room

Minoshin
S/he is comfortable.

Gichi-ojiig
Big Dipper
(Great Fisher)

Apabiwin
Chair

Ayekozi
S/he is tired.

Gichi-dibaakonigewinan
The Seven Grandfather
Teachings

Mazinaakizon
Picture

Gawishimo
S/he goes to bed.

Dibiki-giizis
Moon

Anaakan
Rug

HOW TO MAKE A DREAM CATCHER

You will need:

- 1 wood or metal hoop, 5 to 8 inches (13 to 20 cm) in diameter

- Craft glue, e.g. Elmer's

- 2 yards (1.8 m) of leather or buckskin suede lace, cut into ¼-inch (6 mm)-wide strips

- 1.5 to 2 yards (1 to 1.8 m) hemp, nylon string, yarn, silk thread, or pieces of the raffia plant

- Beads, feathers, and any other materials that are meaningful to you

1. Coat both sides of the hoop generously with glue and wrap the lace around the hoop, moving slowly but tightly until the entire hoop is covered with the lace. Press down as you go to make sure everything sticks. Let the glue fully dry before moving on to the next step.

2. Tie a knot with the string at the top of the hoop. Then, working clockwise, pull the string tightly and wrap it at quarter-hoop intervals, so when you're done with the first revolution you've created a square within the hoop.

3. Once you have created the square, continue making smaller and smaller squares within each square, keeping the pattern symmetrical, or you can weave in a more irregular pattern. The pattern you choose to make is completely up to you

4. When you're done weaving, knot the string to keep your design in place, and then create a loop from which you will hang your dream catcher. Then, on the opposite side (the bottom), use the string to tie on the beads, feathers, and other decorations.

5. Hang your dream catcher above your bed to catch bad dreams. Make sure it is in a place where in the morning the sun will shine on it and burn the bad dreams away.

TRADITIONAL OPTION

The materials above can be found at any craft store, but you can also make a more traditional dream catcher by using 18 to 36 inches (45 to 91 cm) of red willow or any other flexible twig to create the hoop, along with 1.5 to 2 yards (1 to 1.8 m) of twine or sinew.

If you can harvest these materials responsibly, replace step #1 with the following: Bend the red willow branch into a circle and tie the ends together with twine.

ABOUT THE AUTHOR

Descendent of Turtle Mountain **James Vukelich Kaagegaabaw** is a renowned international speaker, author, educator, and social media personality who shares indigenous wisdom for a life well-lived. As the creator of Ojibwe Word of the Day, James is recognized as a leading voice on the interconnectedness of language and culture. His keen insights have developed by speaking with and recording elders and native language speakers across North America as part of the Ojibwe Language Dictionary Project.

For over twenty years, James has facilitated community language tables, consulted with public and private organizations on language and cultural programs, and traveled internationally as a keynote speaker. In addition to publications, he has been featured on numerous podcasts, radio shows, and television programs. James is a passionate advocate for sharing how to live a life of *mino-bimaadiziwin*, the good life. He lives in the Twin Cities, Minnesota with his wife and son.

ABOUT THE ILLUSTRATOR

Marcus Trujillo (he/him) is an enrolled tribal member with the Pueblo of Laguna, one of twenty three sovereign nations located in New Mexico. Marcus is a graphic designer and illustrator who is driven to give back to his community through visual art as a creative passion. Marcus earned a bachelor's degree from the University of New Mexico (UNM), and currently contributes his skill-sets to the Department of Education in Laguna Pueblo. Marcus also contributes his talents to freelance and contract work for various Indigenous-led organizations, businesses, and individuals.

Additionally, Marcus centers kid-lit illustration as a main focus to reach children through picture books and language learning materials. This work is meaningful to Marcus because he believes that true visual representation of Indigenous communities can respectfully take place through culturally accurate understandings. Follow Marcus at haatzeedesigns.com and @haatzeedesigns.

TO JACK

Niizhoo-bines, I'm forever grateful for the time we spent together during these early years. I hope we can always read this book with fond memories of that beautiful time in our lives.

First published in 2024 by becker&mayer!kids, an imprint of The Quarto Group, 142 West 36th Street, 4th Floor, New York, NY 10018, USA
(212) 779-4972 www.Quarto.com

becker&mayer!kids titles are also available at discount for retail, wholesale, promotional, and bulk purchase. For details, contact the Special Sales Manager by email at specialsales@quarto.com or by mail at The Quarto Group, Attn: Special Sales Manager, 100 Cummings Center Suite 265D, Beverly, MA 01915 USA.

10 9 8 7 6 5 4 3 2 1

ISBN: 978-0-7603-8719-1

Digital edition published in 2024
eISBN: 978-0-7603-8720-7

Library of Congress Control Number: 2024936826

Group Publisher: Rage Kindelsperger
Creative Director: Laura Drew
Managing Editor: Cara Donaldson
Cover and Interior Design: Scott Richardson
Illustrations: Marcus Trujillo

Printed in China

Lexile® 660L